THE TRICKY RIDDLES BOOK FOR SMART KIDS

320

FUN RIDDLES, BRAIN TEASERS AND TRICK QUESTIONS

FOR EVERYDAY FAMILY FUN THAT BOOSTS BRAIN POWER

Riddle Me This!

320 brain-tickling riddles for kids
and the whole family

A SPECIAL GIFT FOR OUR READERS

As a special thank you for getting this book, we'd like to give you:

THE SPECIAL BONUS BOOK OF RIDDLES

40 tricky riddles that range from easy to super challenging, and ones that will keep the kids (and grownups) entertained for even longer, while boosting brain power too.

Visit www.daddilife.com/bonusriddles to get yours

Table of contents

CHAPTER ONE

THE ADVANTAGES OF RIDDLING

INTRODUCTION

What has a bottom at the top? (Answer at the end of the chapter)

Welcome to the land of the riddle! Riddles are super fun for kids. And adults. And the ancient Egyptians, Greek philosophers, Batman, King Solomon, Alice (from Wonderland)... even Hobittses! Everyone loves a good riddle.

Did you know besides being fun, regular riddling has huge benefits for your brain?

It's a kind of mental gymnastics that gets your brain thinking in highly creative ways. With each riddle, you widen your brains boundaries, strengthen your ability to focus, and problem solve quicker. These skills are so vital in today's world.

Riddles date back thousands of years. Over 4000 years ago, the ancient Sumerians amused their kids with this cracker: ""There is a house. One enters it blind and comes out seeing. What is it?" Can you guess the answer? It's at the end of this chapter!

Probably the most famous of all riddles in history is the "Riddle of The Sphinx", which was written in the 5th century BC. It's a clever one! - "What goes on four legs in the morning, on two legs at noon, and on three legs in the evening?" This riddle's answer is also at the end of this chapter!

Another famous riddle was written by Lewis Carroll in the book "Alice in Wonderland". On Alice's adventures, she comes across The Mad Hatter, and he challenges her with a riddle - "Why is a raven like a writing desk?" Don't spend too long thinking about this one...there is no answer! It was a trick!

In recent times, the riddle has been made popular by one of Batman's most famous villains - The Riddler. Dressed in a suit full of question marks, his signature move was to present Batman with difficult riddles - and of course, the stakes were high! It's a good thing that Batman was a good riddle-solver. He always worked them out just in time. Here are some of our favorites from The Riddler:

Riddle: what is everywhere, but nowhere, except where something is?

Answer: nothing

Riddle: What is always on its way here, but never arrives?

Answer: Tomorrow

Riddle: How many sides does a circle have?

Answer: Two. The inside and the outside.

In this book, we've compiled 320 brain-tickling riddles to get your kids (and you too!) thinking. They are divided into 3 chapters, each increasing in difficulty. So jump in, with the best of luck from us! Have fun!

* * Answers to above riddles:

Riddle: What has a bottom at the top?

Answer: Your legs!

Riddle: There is a house. One enters it blind and comes out seeing. What is it?

Answer: A school!

Riddle: What goes on four legs in the morning, on two legs at noon, and on three legs in the evening?

Answer: A human. Humans crawl on hands and knees ("four legs") as a baby, walk on two legs in mid-life (representing "noon,") and use a walking stick or cane ("three legs") in old age.

CHAPTER TWO

THE ADVANTAGES OF RIDDLING

It turns out that riddles are far more than just fun. Research has shown that they're really really good for children's brains. Working out riddles helps support children's problem solving, logic, and critical thinking skills. The nature of the riddle is that it requires time to think of the answer, and this exercises the "muscle" of a child's brain - teaching them that mental effort can result in a reward. Where riddles differ from other kinds of problem-solving challenges is that their answers are fun, and perhaps most importantly, it doesn't feel like academics. It's a sneaky education in disguise!

Although riddles have been around for thousands and thousands of years, they have never been more relevant that in today's times. The skills required for many careers are changing. For most of history, careers required a literal education. But today, and likely even more so when your children become adults, we are required to think more like entrepreneurs. Success today often requires strong creative thinking skills. The ability to see solutions where no-one else does, is what all of today's leaders have in common. Traditional education still needs to catch up to this modern skill requirement. And one of the best ways you can fill that educational gap is by introducing your child to riddles!

Regular riddle-solving has been proved to actually increase IQ. Research by the University of Michigan, even found that riddle-solving can increase IQ by up to 4 points!

Riddles also teach kids to pay careful attention to detail. An ability to pick up on minor details, helps in every aspect of our lives. When we're more detailed oriented and precise, the quality of our work improves.

Riddles can even help with your child's social skills. Particularly in the area of developing their sense of humour - as humour shares many of the same elements as riddle-solving, such as playing with words and their meanings.

Finally, riddling can be great for creating bonds. When you are sharing and solving riddles with children, it gives them an opportunity to bond with you and stay connected.

CHAPTER THREE

HOW TO BE A MASTER OF RIDDLES!

What is black and white and red all over?

Let's get into the riddle groove and take a look at how to guide your child in ways to approach riddle-solving. In this book, we've broken up the riddles into 3 levels:

Level 1: Easy Riddles,

Level 2: A Little Less Easy, and

Level 3: "Genius" Level.

Genius level requires extra creative thinking, but it is still possible for children to reach the right answers.

Riddles use regular devices to trick the brain. These often include words or phrases with multiple meanings, metaphors, shifts of perspective, and ambiguities. The most common is the "homophone" - a word that when pronounced, can mean another word (even if it is not spelt the same).

An example of a homophone in a riddle is the example at the start of this chapter. What is black and white and red all over?

The answer requires you to spot that the word "red" sounds the same as "read". Once they've made that step, they can then think of what could be black and white and read all over? The answer? A book! Or a Newspaper! Sometimes there is more than one answer. No matter how ridiculous your child's answer might be, if it makes logical sense, then in fact it should be rewarded with extra points! For example, one child's creative answer for this question was...a sunburnt zebra! She's gonna go far in life!

Working out the answer to riddles is meant to be challenging. Go through our list of riddles and choose those that you feel your child would be able to solve. Consider their age, their level of comprehension, and also their level of vocabulary. Avoid frustrating them with a riddle they're unlikely to be able to solve. Children should experience the joy of reaching a correct answer after some focused thinking. In some cases, you can help your child work through the problem by prompting them with questions that guide them to think in different ways. The most important educational element of challenging your child with riddles, is the opportunity to show them how to approach a problem that needs to be solved.
It can be a great idea to offer a riddle in exchange for a reward. Want the WiFi password? Here's a riddle!

So, without further ado...let's dive in!

CHAPTER FOUR

LEVEL ONE RIDDLES: EASY RIDDLES!

1. What has hands but doesn't clap?

____

2. What has many keys but can't open a single lock?

____

3. I follow you all the time and copy your every move, but you can't touch me or catch me. What am I?

____

4. There's a one-story house in which everything is yellow. Yellow walls, yellow doors, yellow furniture. What color are the stairs?

____

5. What gets wet while drying?

____

6. I have branches, but no fruit, trunk, or leaves. What am I?

____

7. I'm tall when I'm young, and I'm short when I'm old. What am I?

8. What goes up but never comes down?

9. A man who was outside in the rain without an umbrella or hat didn't get a single hair on his head wet. Why?

10. What can you break, even if you never pick it up or touch it?

11. What is full of holes but still holds water?

____

12. What is always in front of you but can't be seen?

____

13. What can't talk but will reply when spoken to?

____

14. The more of this there is, the less you see. What is it?

____

15. What has to be broken before you can use it?

____

16. What is black when it's clean and white when it's dirty?

____

17. What gets bigger when more is taken away?

____

18. I shave every day, but my beard stays the same. What am I?

19. What can you keep after giving to someone?

20. You see a boat filled with people, yet there isn't a single person on board. How is that possible?

21. I'm light as a feather, yet the strongest person can't hold me for five minutes. What am I?

____

22. What month of the year has 28 days?

____

23. Where does today come before yesterday?

____

24. If you've got me, you want to share me; if you share me, you haven't kept me. What am I?

____

25. What goes up and down but doesn't move?

____

26. David's parents have three sons: Snap, Crackle, and what's the name of the third son?

____

27. What can you hold in your left hand but not in your right?

28. It belongs to you, but other people use it more than you do. What is it?

29. What has lots of eyes, but can't see?

30. What has legs but doesn't walk?

31. What has one head, one foot, and four legs?

32. You walk into a room that contains a match, a kerosene lamp, a candle, and a fireplace. What would you light first?

____

33. What has words but never speaks?

____

34. What runs all around a backyard yet never moves?

____

35. What has one eye but can't see?

____

36. What has many needles but doesn't sew?

____

37. What can you catch but not throw?

____

38. What can travel all around the world without leaving its corner?

39. What has a thumb and four fingers, but is not a hand?

40. What has a head and a tail but no body?

41. What tastes better than it smells?

42. What has 13 hearts, but no other organs?

43. It stalks the countryside with ears that can't hear. What is it?

44. What kind of coat is best put on wet?

45. What has a bottom at the top?

46. What has four wheels and flies?

47. Two fathers and two sons are in a car, yet there are only three people in the car. How?

48. If there are three apples and you take away two, how many apples do you have?

49. What five-letter word becomes shorter when you add two letters to it?

50. What can't be put in a saucepan?

51. What begins with an "e" and only contains one letter?

52. You see me once in June, twice in November, and not at all in May. What am I?

53. What is so fragile that saying its name breaks it?

54. Forward I am heavy, but backward I am not. What am I?

55. What can fill a room but takes up no space?

56. Come up and we go, drop and we stay. What am I?

57. What four-letter word can be written forward, backwards, or upside down, and can still be read from left to right?

58. A girl has as many brothers as sisters, but each brother has only half as many brothers as sisters. How many brothers and sisters are there in the family?

59. What is cut on a table but is never eaten?

60. Mary has four daughters, and each of her daughters has a brother. How many children does Mary have?

61. What can run but never walks, has a mouth but never talks, has a head but never weeps, has a bed but never sleeps?

62. What has many teeth, but can't bite?

63. If you drop me, I'm sure to crack, but give me a smile and I'll always smile back. What am I?

64. What kind of band never plays music?

65. I am an odd number. Take away a letter and I become even. What number am I?

66. I am always hungry and will die if not fed, but whatever I touch will soon turn red. What am I?

67. What is easy to get into but hard to get out of?

68. What word is pronounced the same if you take away four of its five letters?

69. With pointed fangs I sit and wait; with piercing force I crunch out fate; grabbing victims, proclaiming might; physically joining with a single bite. What am I?

70. What has eyes, a tongue, and a soul but can't see, taste, or die?

71. I have lakes with no water, mountains with no stone, and cities with no buildings. What am I?

72. I go up and down stairs without moving. What am I?

73. If a red house is made of red bricks, and a yellow house is made of yellow bricks, what is a greenhouse made of?

74. I am a word of letters three; add two and fewer there will be. What word am I?

75. Three doctors said that Bill was their brother. Bill says he has no brothers. How many brothers does Bill actually have?

76. What does man love more than life, hate more than death or mortal strife; that which contented men desire; the poor have, the rich require; the miser spends, the spendthrift saves, and all men carry to their graves?

77. When things go wrong, what can you always count on?

78. Mr. Blue lives in the blue house. Mrs. Yellow lives in the yellow house. Mr. Orange lives in the orange house. Who lives in the White House?

79. The person who makes it has no need for it; the person who buys it has no use for it. The person who uses it can neither see nor feel it. What is it?

____

80. Which is heavier: a ton of bricks or a ton of feathers?

____

81. What goes through cities and fields, but never moves?

____

82. A word I know, six letters it contains, remove one letter and 12 remains, what is it?

____

83. What happens once in a lifetime, twice in a moment, but never in one hundred years?

____

84. What goes in your pocket but keeps it empty?

____

85. I sometimes run but cannot walk. You follow me around. What am I?

____

86. How can a leopard change its spots?

____

87. What word is spelled wrong in the dictionary?

____

88. A man looks at a painting in a museum and says, "Brothers and sisters, I have none, but that man's father is my father's son." Who is in the painting?

____

89. What bank never has any money?

____

90. I am so simple that I can only point, yet I guide men all over the world.

91. I can rush, I can be hot, I can be cold, I can be hard, I can slip through anything. What am I?

92. I can be good for you; I can be bad. You can find me all over your body. What am I?

93. What has four eyes but can't see?

94. What has a neck but no head?

95. A phone and case cost $110 in total. The phone costs $100 more than the case. How much is the phone?

96. What breaks yet never falls, and what falls yet never breaks?

____

97. People make me, save me, change me, raise me. What am I?

____

98. I turn once, what is out will not get in. I turn again, what is in will not get out. What am I?

____

99. The more you take, the more you leave behind. What are they?

____

100. What building has the most stories?

____

101. What kind of ship has two mates but no captain?

____

102. You're running a race and at the very end, you pass the person in 2nd place. What place did you finish the race in?

____

103. It's raining at midnight, but the forecast for tomorrow and the next day is clear. Will there be sunny weather in 48 hours?

____

104. What can go up a chimney down, but can't go down a chimney up?

____

105. It has keys, but no locks. It has space, but no room. You can enter, but can't go inside. What is it?

____

106. You will buy me to eat but never eat me. What am I?

____

107. What can jump higher than a building?

____

108. I make a loud sound when I'm changing. When I do change, I get bigger but weigh less. What am I?

109. Sarah has a very big family. She has 20 aunts, 20 uncles, and 50 cousins. Each of her cousins has an aunt who is not Sarah's aunt. How is this possible?

110. A cowboy comes into town on Friday. He stays two nights at a local hotel. He leaves on Friday. How is this possible?

111. What's the capital of France?

112. A bus driver was heading down a busy street in the city. He went past three stop signs without stopping, went the wrong way down a one-way street, and answered a message on his phone. But the bus driver didn't break any traffic laws. How?

113. Imagine you are in a room with no windows or doors. How will you get out?

114. I have wings, I am able to fly, I'm not a bird, yet I soar high in the sky. What am I?

115. What falls in winter but never gets hurt?

116. Where does Friday come before Thursday?

117. What is orange in color, green on top, and sounds like a parrot?

118. What invention lets you look right through a wall?

119. What word contains 26 letters, but only has three syllables?

120. A girl fell off a 20-foot ladder. She wasn't hurt. Why?

121. I add lots of flavor and have many layers, but if you get too close I'll make you cry. What am I?

122. What kind of cup doesn't hold water?

123. I have to be opened, but I don't have a lid or a key to get in. What am I?

124. What can you hear, but not see or touch, even though you control it?

____

125. What runs but never gets tired?

____

126. What has stripes and goes through the air?

____

127. If you threw a yellow stone into a blue sea, what would it become?

____

128. What begins with T ends with T and has a T in it?

____

129. If an electric train is traveling 60 MPH and going against the wind, which way will the train's smoke drift?

____

130. How do you make the number "one" disappear?

131. What is as big as a hippo but weighs nothing at all?

132. I can be cracked or played, told or made.
What am I?

133. When is "L" greater than "XL"?

134. What's black and white and read all over?

135. I give you one, and you have two or none.
What am I?

136. What do you find at the end of a rainbow?

137. What falls a lot but doesn't get hurt at all?

138. What vehicle is spelled the same backwards and forwards?

139. What starts with a P, ends with an E, and has thousands of letters?

140. There were two ducks in front of a duck, two ducks behind a duck, and one duck in the middle. How many ducks were there in total?

---

141. A man was driving a black truck. His lights were not on. The moon was not out. A lady was crossing the street. How did the man see her?

---

142. During which month do people sleep the least?

---

143. A man dies of old age on his 25 birthday. How is this possible?

---

144. What word in the English language does the following: The first two letters signify a male, the first three letters signify a female, the first four letters signify a great, while the entire world signifies a great woman. What is the word?

---

145. Not many people have stepped on me. I never stay full for long. I have a dark side. What am I?

____

146. If two's a company, and three's a crowd, what are four and five?

____

147. Almost everyone needs it, asks for it, gives it, but almost nobody takes it. What is it?

____

148. What is black when you buy it, red when you use it, and white when you are done with it?

____

149. What is made of water, but if you put it into water it will die?

____

150. What loses its head in the morning and gets it back at night?

____

LEVEL ONE ANSWERS

1. A clock.
2. A piano.
3. Your shadow.
4. There aren't any–it's a one-story house.
5. A towel.
6. A bank.
7. A candle.
8. Your age.
9. He was bald.
10. A promise.
11. A sponge.
12. The future.
13. An echo.
14. Darkness.
15. An egg.
16. A chalkboard.
17. A hole.
18. A barber.
19. Your word.
20. All the people on the boat are married.
21. Your breath.
22. All of them!
23. The dictionary.
24. A secret.
25. A staircase.
26. David.
27. Your right elbow.
28. Your name.
29. A potato.
30. A table.

31. A bed.
32. The match.
33. A book.
34. A fence.
35. A needle.
36. A Christmas tree.
37. A cold.
38. A stamp.
39. A glove.
40. A coin.
41. Your tongue.
42. A deck of cards.
43. Corn.
44. A coat of paint.
45. Your legs.
46. A garbage truck.
47. They are a grandfather, father, and son.
48. You have two apples.
49. Short.
50. Its lid.
51. An envelope.
52. The letter "e."
53. Silence.
54. The word "ton."
55. Light.
56. An anchor.
57. NOON.
58. Four sisters and three brothers.
59. A deck of cards.
60. Five–each daughter has the same brother.

61. A river.
62. A comb.
63. A mirror.
64. A rubber band.
65. Seven
66. Fire.
67. Trouble.
68. Queue.
69. A stapler.
70. A shoe.
71. A map.
72. A carpet.
73. Glass. All greenhouses are made of glass.
74. Few.
75. None. He has three sisters.
76. Nothing.
77. Your fingers.
78. The president.
79. A coffin.
80. Neither–they both weigh a ton.
81. A road.
82. Dozens.
83. The letter "M."
84. A hole.
85. Your nose.
86. By moving from one spot to another.
87. Wrong.
88. The man's son.
89. A river bank.
90. A compass.

91. Water.
92. Bacteria.
93. Mississippi.
94. A bottle.
95. $105.
96. Day and night.
97. Money.
98. A key.
99. Footsteps.
100. The library.
101. A relationship.
102. You finished in 2nd place.
103. No, it won't be sunny because it will be dark out. In 48 hours, it will be midnight again.
104. An umbrella. If your umbrella is "down," it can fit through a chimney, but if it's "up," it won't fit!
105. A keyboard.
106. A plate.
107. Anything that can jump – buildings don't jump!
108. Popcorn.
109. Their aunt is Sarah's mom!
110. His horse's name is Friday.
111. The letter "F." It's the only capital letter in France.
112. He was walking, not driving.
113. Stop imagining.
114. An airplane.
115. Snow.
116. In the dictionary.
117. A carrot.
118. A window.
119. Alphabet.

120. She fell off the bottom step.
121. An onion.
122. A hiccup
123. An egg.
124. Your voice.
125. A water faucet.
126. A basketball.
127. Wet.
128. A teapot.
129. There is no smoke from an electric train.
130. Add a "g" and it is "gone."
131. A hippo's shadow.
132. A joke.
133. When you use Roman numerals.
134. A newspaper.
135. A choice.
136. The letter W.
137. Rain.
138. Racecar.
139. The Post Office.
140. Three.
141. It was a bright, sunny day.
142. February (as February has fewer nights, of course!).
143. He was born on February 29.
144. Heroine.
145. The moon.
146. Nine.
147. Advice.
148. Charcoal.
149. An ice cube.
150. A pillow.

CHAPTER FIVE

LEVEL TWO: A LITTLE LESS EASY RIDDLES!

1. What question can you never answer yes to?

---

2. What has six faces but does not wear makeup, and twenty-one eyes but cannot see?

---

3. What is 3/7 chicken, 2/3 cat, and 2/4 goat?

---

4. All 5 sisters are busy. Ann is reading a book, Rose is cooking, Katy is playing chess, and Mary is doing the laundry. What is the 5th sister doing?

---

5. What is the last thing you take off before bed?

---

6. I come from a mine but always get surrounded by wood. Everyone uses me. What am I?

---

7. Ben owns a pet store. He puts one canary per cage, but has one bird too many. If he puts two canaries in each cage, he has one cage too many. How many cages and canaries does he have?

8. Before Mt. Everest was discovered, what was the tallest mountain peak in the world?

9. The answer I give is yes, but what I mean is no. What was the question?

10. A man calls his dog from the opposite side of a river. The dog crosses the river without a bridge or a boat and manages to not get wet. How is this possible?

11. First, think of the color of clouds. Next, think of the color of snow. Now, think of the color of a full bright moon. What do cows drink?

____

12. Which English verb becomes past tense just by rearranging the letters?

____

13. Different lights make me strange by changing me into different sizes. What am I?

____

14. I am something people love or hate. I change people's appearances and thoughts. If a person takes care of themselves, I will go up even higher. Some people might want to try and hide me, but I will show. No matter how hard people try, I will never go down. What am I?

____

15. How can you physically stand behind your father if he is standing behind you?

____

16. Lighter than what I am made of, more of me is hidden than is seen. What am I?

____

17. What has no beginning, end, or middle?

____

18. Paul's height is six feet, he's an assistant at a butcher's shop, and wears size 9 shoes. What does he weigh?

____

19. A is the brother of B. B is the brother of C. C is the father of D. So, how is D related to A?

____

20. Without the first two letters, I'm an intelligent animal. Without the first three letters, I'm a subject in school. And, without the first four letters, I'm the letter "e." What am I?

____

21. You start at red and stop at green. What am I?

____

22. It has five wheels, though often thought of as four, but you cannot use it without that one more. What is it?

____

23. My thunder comes before the lightning; my lightning comes before clouds; my rain dries all the land it touches. What am I?

____

24. A plane crashed between the border of Canada and America. Where do you bury the survivors?

____

25. First you eat me, and then you get eaten. What am I?

____

26. It's shorter than the rest, but when you're happy, you raise it up like it's the best. What is it?

27. Spelled forward I'm what you do every day, spelled backward I'm something you hate. What am I?

28. When is a door no longer a door?

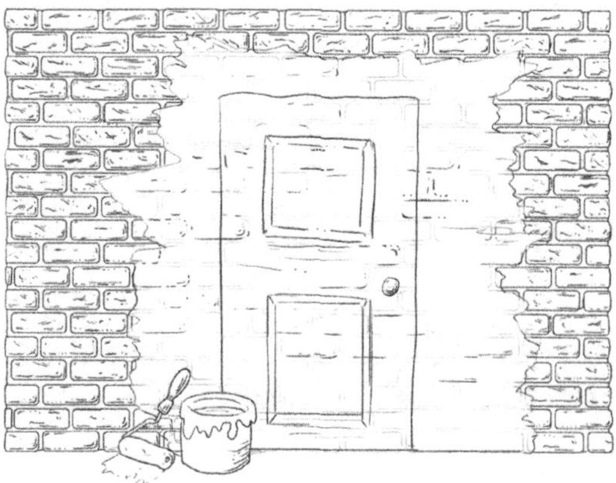

29. If your uncle's sister is not your aunt, what relation is she to you?

30. How far can you walk into the forest?

31. How high do you have to count before you use the letter "a" in the English spelling of the whole number?

____

32. What type of cheese is made backward?

____

33. Until I am measured, I am not known. Yet how you miss me when I have flown. What am I?

____

34. What are the next three letters in this combination: OTTFFSS?

____

35. What's mine that only you can have?

____

36. A man is trapped in a room. The room has only two possible exits: two doors. Through the first door, there is a room constructed from magnifying glasses. The blazing hot sun instantly fries anything or anyone that enters. Through the second door, there is a fire-breathing dragon. How does the man escape?

____

37. What is next in this sequence? JFMAMJJASON

____

38. Two in a corner, 1 in a room, 0 in a house, but 1 in a shelter. What am I?

____

39. A girl is sitting in a house at night that has no lights on at all. There is no lamp, no candle, nothing. Yet she is reading. How?

____

40. Anna drank two-thirds cup of wine, and Charlotte drank a fourth cup of wine. Who drank the most?

____

41. Five pieces of coal, a carrot, and a scarf are lying on the lawn. Nobody put them on the lawn, but there is a perfectly logical reason why they should be there. What is it?

42. My first is in chocolate but not in ham, my second's in cake and also in jam, my third at tea-time is easily found, my whole is a friend who's often around. What am I?

43. How can a man go 8 days without sleep?

44. Some people prefer being on top, others prefer being on the bottom, and it always involves a bed. What am I?

45. While a cat was outside, it started to downpour. The cat couldn't find any shelter and got completely soaked by the rain, yet not a single hair was wet. How could this be

____

46. What stays where it is even after it goes off?

____

47. What has ten letters and starts with gas?

____

48. What occurs once in a minute, twice in a moment, and never in one thousand years?

____

49. Three different doctors said that Paul is their brother yet Paul claims he has no brothers. Who is lying?

____

50. When you look for something, why is it always in the last place you look?

____

51. How can you throw a ball as hard as you can only to have it come back to you without it bouncing off of anything?

____

52. A monkey, a squirrel, and a bird are racing to the top of a coconut tree. Who gets to the banana first; the monkey, the squirrel, or the bird?

____

53. Which will burn longer: the candles on the birthday cake of a boy or the candles on the birthday cake of a girl?

____

54. Two girls were born to the same mother, on the same day, at the same time, in the same month and year, and yet they're not twins. How can this be?

____

55. How can you drop a raw egg on the concrete floor without cracking it?

____

56. I possess a halo of water, walls of stone, and a tongue of wood. Long I have stood; what am I?

____

57. When does 11+3=2?

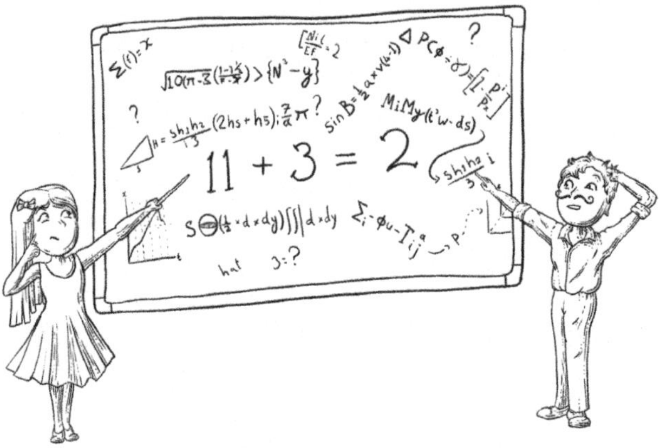

____

58. You always find me in the past, I can be created in the present, but the future can never taint me. What am I?

____

59. Soldiers line up, spaced with pride, two long rows lined side by side, one sole unit can decide if the rows will unite or divide. What is it?

____

60. A man is asked what his daughters look like. He answers, "they are all blondes, but two, all brunettes, but two, and all redheads, but two." How many daughters does he have?

61. What has roots that no one sees and looms much taller than trees? Up it goes but yet it never grows; what is it?

62. Your friends make a surprise visit to your house early one morning. So, you decide to make breakfast for everyone. You start to gather the ingredients you need for pancakes. Then you get juice from the refrigerator to serve as well. What do you open first?

63. Two people are born at the same moment, but they don't have the same birthdays. How?

64. We hurt without moving and poison without touching. We bear truth and lies but are not judged by size. What are we?

65. Which English word is the odd one out: Stun, Ton, Evil, Letter, Mood, Bad, Strap, Snap, and Straw?

66. I promise, I offend, I direct, and I fight. What am I?

67. I fly without wings and cry without eyes. Wherever I lead, darkness follows. What could I be?

68. Why is Europe like a frying pan?

69. How many of each species did Moses take on the ark with him?

70. A king, a queen, and two twins all lay in a large room. How are there no adults in the room?

71. Why can't we take a picture of a man with a wooden leg?

72. What do you call a chihuahua in the summer?

73. I am a five-letter word. I sound the same when you remove my first letter. I sound the same when you remove my third letter. I sound the same when my last letter is removed, and I sound the same when all three are removed. What word am I?

74. What has two humps and is found at the North Pole?

75. I am born tall and grow short with age. What could I be?

76. Jeff is younger than Rodney but older than Debbie. Larry is older than Erica who is older than Jeff. Rodney is older than Larry. Who is the middle child?

77. You throw away the outside, eat the inside, then throw away the inside. What is it?

78. Turn me on my side and I am everything. Cut me in half and I am nothing. What am I?

79. I'm so fast you can't see me, though everyone else can see straight through me. I don't stop until the day you die. What am I?

80. I don't have eyes, but once I did see. Once I had thoughts, but now I'm white and empty.

81. What flies without wings?

82. He has married many women, but has never been married. Who am I?

83. A girl was ten on her last birthday, and will be twelve on her next birthday. How is this possible?

84. I love to dance and twist and prance, I shake my tail, as away I sail, wingless I fly into the sky. What am I?

85. What number do you get when you multiply all of the numbers on a telephone's number pad?

86. Thousands lay up gold within this house, But no man made it. Many guard this house, But no man wants it. What is it?

87. What word looks the same upside down and backwards?

88. What is precious in a pack of cards?

89. Tear one off and scratch my head, what once was red is black instead?

90. How do you fix a cracked pumpkin?

91. Is an older one-hundred-dollar bill worth more than a newer one?

92. What is it that no man ever yet did see, which never was, but always is to be?

93. What is that which goes with a car, comes with a car, is of no use to a car, and yet the car cannot go without it?

94. I have a big mouth, and I am also quite loud! I am NOT a gossip but I do get involved with everyone's dirty business. What am I?

95. I have an eye but am blind, a sea, but no water; a bee, but no honey; Tea but no coffee; and a why, but no answer. What am I?

____

96. This old one runs forever, but never moves at all. He has no lungs nor throat, but still a mighty roaring call. What is it?

____

97. What is it that after you take away the whole, some still remains?

____

98. What body part is pronounced as one letter but written with three, only two different letters are used?

____

99. What's the difference between here and there?

____

100. What is unusual about the following words: revive, banana, grammar, voodoo, assess, potato, dresser, uneven?

____

101. You can tumble in it, roll in it, burn it. Animals eat it, use it to cover floors, and it is still used beyond stall doors. It freshens whatever it is placed on, and absorbs whatever is poured into it. What is it?

102. What can be swallowed but can swallow you also?

103. What always goes to bed with its shoes on?

104. There is a bomb on top of a computer; around the computer are a hairbrush, keys, phone and a cup. When the explosion comes, what item destroyed first?

105. Tool of a thief, toy of a queen. Always used to be unseen. Sign of joy, sign of sorrow. Giving all likeness borrowed. What am I?

106. What has a neck but no head, no arms, and no hands?

107. If you journey without it, you will never prevail, but if you have too much of it you will surely fail. What is it?

108. I cannot hear or even see, but sense light and sounds there may be. Sometimes I end up on the hook, or even deep into a book. What am I?

109. Hands she has but does not hold, teeth she has but does not bite, feet she has but they are cold, eyes she has but without sight. Who is she?

____

110. At the sound of me, men may dream. Or stamp their feet at the sound of me, women may laugh or sometimes weep. What am I?

____

111. Inside a burning house, this thing is best to make. And best to make it quickly, before the fire's too much to take! What is it?

____

112. I can bring tears to your eyes; resurrect the dead, make you smile, and reverse time. I form in an instant, but I last a lifetime. What am I?

____

113. Everyone has me but nobody can lose me. What am I?

____

114. Teddy bears are never hungry because they are always what?

115. I am the only organ that named myself. What am I?

116. What kind of dog keeps the best time?

117. Looks like water, but it's heat. Sits on sand, lays on concrete. People have been known to follow it everywhere. But it gets them no place, And all they can do is stare. What am I?

118. You use a knife to slice my head and weep beside me when I am dead. What am I?

119. What asks but never answers?

120. You can easily touch me, but not see me. You can throw me out, but not away.

121. What do you get when you cross an automobile with a household animal?

122. What has a ring, but no finger?

123. An open-ended barrel, I am shaped like a hive. I am filled with the flesh, and the flesh is alive! What am I?

124. I have a face, two arms, and two hands, yet I can not move. I count to twelve, yet I can not speak. I can still tell you something every day.

125. What calls for help, when written in capital letters, is the same forwards, backwards and upside down?

126. What is made of wood, but can't be sawed?

127. What doesn't get any wetter, no matter how much rain falls on it?

128. When they are caught, they are thrown away. When they escape, you itch all day. What are they?

129. What is higher without the head, than with it?

130. Your mother's brother's only brother-in-law is asleep on your couch. Who is asleep on your couch?

131. Never resting, never still. Moving silently from hill to hill. It does not walk, run or trot. All is cool where it is not.

132. When asked how old she was, Suzie replied, "in two years I will be twice as old as I was five years ago." How old is she?

133. Where everyone wants to run home and stealing is encouraged.

134. This is needed both for courage and hardcover books.

---

135. I cover what's real, hide what is true, but sometimes bring out the courage in you. What am I?

---

136. What has no beginning, end, or middle?

---

137. I have two arms, but fingers none. I have two feet, but cannot run. I carry well, but I have found I carry best with my feet off the ground. What am I?

---

138. Though liquid in nature, don't push me too far for then I will break, and the damage may scar. What am I?

---

139. You can do this with your friends. You can do this with your nose. But don't do it with your friend's nose!

140. What turns everything around, but does not move?

LEVEL TWO ANSWERS

1. Are you asleep yet?"
2. Dice.
3. Chicago.
4. Playing chess with Katy!
5. Your feet from the floor.
6. Pencil lead.
7. Ben has 3 cages and 4 canaries
8. It was still Mt. Everest.
9. "Do you mind?"
10. The river was frozen.
11. Water.
12. "Eat" which can turn into "ate."
13. The pupil of an eye.
14. Age.
15. You and your father are back-to-back.
16. An iceberg.
17. A doughnut.
18. Meat.
19. A is D's uncle.
20. Grape.
21. A watermelon.
22. A car.
23. A volcano.
24. They are survivors, you don't bury them.
25. A fishhook.
26. A thumb.
27. Live.
28. When it's ajar.
29. Your mother.
30. Halfway. After that, you're walking out.
31. One thousand.

32. Edam.

33. Time.

34. E N T (eight, nine, and ten).

35. My heart.

36. He waits until night time and then goes through the first door.

37. The letter "D." The sequence contains the first letter of each month.

38. The letter "R."

39. The woman is blind and is reading braille.

40. Charlotte as she drank four cups of wine.

41. They were used by children who made a snowman. The snow has now melted.

42. A cat.

43. He only sleeps at night.

44. A bunk bed.

45. It was a hairless cat.

46. An alarm clock.

47. An automobile.

48. The letter "M."

49. No one is lying because the three doctors are Paul's sisters.

50. Because when you find it, you stop looking!

51. Throw the ball straight into the air.

52. There are no bananas at the top of a coconut tree!

53. No candles burn longer-they all burn shorter.

54. The two babies are two of a set of triplets.

55. The egg won't crack the concrete floor!

56. A castle.

57. On a clock.

58. History.

59. A zip.

60. Three. One is blonde, one is brunette, and one is a redhead.

61. A mountain.

62. First, you open your front door to let your friends inside.

63. They were born in different time zones.

64. Words.

65. "Letter" as it is the only one that does not spell another word when it's written backward.

66. A hand.

67. A cloud.

68. Because it has Greece at the bottom.

69. None. Moses wasn't on the ark. Noah was.

70. They're all beds!

71. The wooden leg is not a camera.

72. A Hot Dog!

73. Empty (empty, emty, emp-t, m-t).

74. A lost camel!

75. A pencil.

76. Erica.

77. Corn on the cob.

78. The number 8. On its side, it looks like the symbol for infinity, and when you cut it in half, it looks like two zeroes.

79. The blink of an eye.

80. A skull.

81. Time.

82. A preacher.

83. Today is her eleventh birthday.

84. A kite.

85. 0 Anything multiplied by 0 will equal 0.

86. A beehive.

87. Swims.

88. Diamonds.

89. A match.

90. With a pumpkin patch.
91. A $100 bill is worth more than a $1 bill (newer one).
92. Tomorrow.
93. Noise.
94. A vacuum cleaner.
95. The alphabet.
96. A waterfall.
97. Wholesome.
98. Eye.
99. The letter "T".
100. Remove the first letter of each word and they are the same backwards.
101. Hay.
102. Pride.
103. A horse.
104. The bomb.
105. A mask.
106. A shirt
107. Confidence.
108. A worm.
109. A doll.
110. Music.
111. Haste.
112. A memory.
113. A shadow.
114. Stuffed.
115. The brain.
116. A watchdog.
117. A mirage.
118. An onion.
119. An owl. (Think of the sound one makes!).
120. Your back.

121. Carpet 'Car' and 'pet.'
122. A phone.
123. A thimble.
124. A clock.
125. SOS.
126. Sawdust.
127. Water.
128. Fleas.
129. A pillow.
130. Your dad.
131. Sunshine.
132. Twelve.
133. Baseball.
134. A spine.
135. Makeup.
136. A circle.
137. A wheelbarrow.
138. Glass.
139. Pick.
140. A mirror.

CHAPTER SIX

LEVEL THREE:

GENIUS-LEVEL RIDDLES!

1. I talk, but I do not speak my mind. I hear words, but I do not listen to thoughts. When I wake, all see me. When I sleep, all hear me. Many heads are on my shoulders. Many hands are at my feet. The strongest steel cannot break my visage, but the softest whisper can destroy me. The quietest whimper can be heard. What am I?

____

2. Voiceless it cries, wingless it flies, toothless bites, and mouthless mutters. What is it?

____

3. This thing all things devours; birds, beasts, trees, flowers; gnaws iron, bites steel; grinds hard stones to meal; slays kings, ruins towns, and beats mountains down. What is it?

____

4. When John was 6 years old, he hammered a nail into his favorite tree to mark his height. Ten years later, at age 16, John returned to see how much higher the nail was. If the tree grew by 5 centimeters each year, how much higher would the nail be?

____

5. There are four brothers in this world that were all born together. The first runs and never wearies. The second eats and is never full. The third drinks and is always thirsty. The fourth sings a song that is never good. What are the four brothers?

6. A man went to town with a fox, a goose, and a sack of corn. He came to a stream he had to cross in a tiny boat. He could only take one across at a time. He could not leave the fox alone with the goose or the goose alone with the corn. How did he get them all safely over the stream?

7. If you're 8 feet away from a door and with each move you advance half the distance to the door. How many moves will it take to reach the door?

____

8. Tim and Mel are long-distance lovers. Tim has just purchased an engagement ring for Mel and wants to mail it to her. Unfortunately the only way to ensure the ring will be received is to place a lock on the package. Tim has locks and Mel has locks but neither have keys for each others locks. How can they ensure the ring isn't stolen?

____

9. I am the part of the bird that is not in the sky, who can drown in the ocean and yet remain dry. A last vestige of man that refuses to die. In mourning I am tossed at your feet to lie; I begin my job early, devouring your ankles and thighs. I work my way up, eating your legs to your waist. And though around midday away I am chased, I return quickly to savor the arm of my taste. As evening falls I enter your lungs, spiraling down past your mouth and your tongue. I feast on your body, your soul, and your mind, but as darkness falls you shall find that away I will go, a relief for some; At least until tomorrow morning comes. What am I?

____

10. An old man wanted to leave all of his money to one of his three sons, but he didn't know which one he should give it to. He gave each of them a few coins and told them to buy something that would be able to fill their living room. The first man bought straw, but there was not enough to fill the room. The second bought some sticks, but they still did not fill the room. The third man bought two things that filled the room, so he obtained his father's fortune. What were the two things that the man bought?

____

11. I am black of eye and bright of hair, and my feet are firmly in the ground. I love the sun upon my face, and I follow it around. When I am dead and gone tis said, that I will droop real low, that I will keep the birds well fed, standing stiff there in my row. What am I?

____

12. I cannot be other than what I am until the man who made me dies. Power and glory will fall to me finally, only when he last closes his eyes. Who am I?

____

13. Sometimes I am loved, usually by the young. Other times I am dreaded, mostly by the old ones. I am hard to remember, also hard to forget. And yet, if you do, you'll make someone upset. I occur every day. Everyone has to face me. Even if you don't want it to happen; embrace me. What am I?

---

14. Inside me the adventurous find quests and treasures of every kind. Trolls, goblins, orcs, and more, await within my closed walls for all those that wish to visit me. Your hands are the key to secrets untold, and your mind will unlock the door. What am I?

---

15. As a whole, I am both safe and secure. Behead me, and I become a place of meeting. Behead me again, and I am the partner of ready. Restore me, and I become the domain of beasts. What am I?

GENIUS-LEVEL ANSWERS!

1. An actor.
2. The wind.
3. Time.
4. The nail would be at the same height since trees grow at their tops.
5. Water, Fire, Earth, and Wind.
6. He took the goose over first and came back. Then, he took the fox across and brought the goose back. Next, he took the corn over. He came back alone and took the goose.
7. You will never reach the door, it will always be half the distance, no matter how small!
8. Tim places a lock on the package and sends it to Mel. Mel places one of her locks on the package and sends it back to Tim. Tim removes his lock and sends the package back to Mel.
9. A shadow.
10. The wise son bought a candle and a box of matches. After lighting the candle, the light filled the entire room.
11. A sunflower.
12. A prince - becomes king when his father dies.
13. A birthday.
14. A book.
15. Stable, table, able, stable.

CHAPTER SEVEN

SUPER SILLY RIDDLES

1. No matter how fast a man walks, what always goes on ahead?

2. What room can you never enter?

3. What do you call a nose with no body?

4. I am a fast cat, but you should never trust me. What am I?

5. Why should you never trust atoms?

6. The world tongue-twister champion just got arrested. What did the judge decide to give him?

7. Do you know what a blind deer is called?

8. People are usually shocked when they find out what I am. What am I?

9. A magician has lost his magic. What is his name?

10. Why is the letter A like a flower?

11. What do you call a flying priest?

12. A man swallowed 100 rabbits. What is his name?

13. Why is the perfect height for a king 12 inches?

14. Bruce Lee was fast, but he had an even faster brother. What was his name?

15. Apple decided to make an iCar. Why did no one buy them?

SUPER SILLY RIDDLE ANSWERS!

1. A hat!
2. A mushroom!
3. Nobody knows!
4. A cheetah!
5. They make up everything!
6. A tough sentence!
7. No idea!
8. A bad electrician!
9. Ian!
10. Because a "b" comes after it!
11. A bird of pray.
12. Warren!
13. It makes a great ruler!
14. Sudden Lee!
15. It didn't have windows!

It's time to get your Riddle Master Certificate.

Did you enjoy the book? We really hope you did. If you think there's riddles that could be even better do write to us to let us know how it could be. We love to hear feedback.

As we're a 100% self-published book, we'd really appreciate if you (or a grown-up) could leave a review on Amazon. When you do, more people will find out about the book. It also lets Amazon know that we're making kids around the world laugh and think, so even few words and ratings would go a long way.

Also before you go - if you have finished the book, then you DESERVE A PRIZE - our Master of Riddles certificate!

All you need to do is send a picture of you with an adult and the book to dad@daddilife.com with the subject "I'm The Master Of Riddles" and we'll send you a personalized copy of your very own to print!

A SPECIAL GIFT FOR OUR READERS

As a special thank you for getting this book, we'd like to give you:

THE SPECIAL BONUS BOOK OF RIDDLES

40 tricky riddles that range from easy to super challenging, and ones that will keep the kids (and grownups) entertained for even longer, while boosting brain power too.

Visit www.daddilife.com/bonusriddles to get yours

Special Thanks and More Riddles!

A special thanks to the DaddiLife Books team, Marc, Emilie and a special thanks to Matthew for his great work!

Facebook Groups

Did you know that as well as this book there are a few different online groups dedicated to creating different riddles each day. Here's two of our favorites that we wanted to share with you to continue your riddle journey.

Genius Brains - https://www.facebook.com/groups/genius.brains/

Riddles and Brain Teasers - https://www.facebook.com/groups/3267048513414988/

Enjoy!

Printed in Great Britain
by Amazon

24729980R00059